The SaaS Prince

kunal gupta, niccolò di bernardo dei machiavelli, & claude sonnet 3.5

CONTENTS

I. OF THE VARIOUS KINDS OF SOFTWARE EMPIRES AND THE MEANS BY WHICH THEY ARE ACQUIRED

II. CONCERNING HEREDITARY SAAS MONARCHIES

III. CONCERNING MIXED SAAS EMPIRES

IV. WHY CERTAIN SAAS ACQUISITIONS DO NOT REBEL AGAINST THEIR NEW OVERLORDS

V. HOW TO GOVERN SAAS FIEFDOMS THAT, PRIOR TO ACQUISITION, LIVED UNDER THEIR OWN LAWS

VI. CONCERNING NEW SAAS PRINCIPALITIES ACQUIRED THROUGH ONE'S OWN INNOVATION AND FORTITUDE

VII. CONCERNING SAAS PRINCIPALITIES ACQUIRED BY FORTUNE OR THE FAVOR OF THE MASSES

VIII. CONCERNING THOSE WHO HAVE OBTAINED SAAS DOMINION BY NEFARIOUS MEANS

IX. CONCERNING THE CIVIL SAAS PRINCIPALITY

X. CONCERNING THE WAY IN WHICH THE STRENGTH OF A SAAS PRINCIPALITY SHOULD BE MEASURED

XI. CONCERNING OPEN SOURCE PRINCIPALITIES

XII. CONCERNING THE VARIOUS KINDS OF DEVELOPMENT FORCES AND OUTSOURCED MERCENARIES

- XIII. CONCERNING AUXILIARY, MIXED, AND NATIVE TECHNOLOGIES
- XIV. THAT WHICH CONCERNS A SAAS PRINCE ON THE SUBJECT OF THE ART OF PRODUCT DEVELOPMENT
- XV. CONCERNING THINGS FOR WHICH SAAS LEADERS AND THEIR PRODUCTS ARE PRAISED OR BLAMED
- XVI. CONCERNING GENEROSITY AND FRUGALITY IN SAAS MODELS
- XVII. CONCERNING USER DELIGHT AND MONETIZATION, AND WHETHER IT IS BETTER TO HAVE A BELOVED PRODUCT OR A PROFITABLE ONE
- XVIII. HOW SAAS PRINCES SHOULD HONOR THEIR WORD
- XIX. THAT ONE SHOULD AVOID BEING DESPISED AND HATED BY ONE'S USERS
- XX. ARE CERTAIN SAAS FEATURES AND STRATEGIES WHICH PRINCES OFTEN EMPLOY USEFUL OR HURTFUL?
- XXI. HOW A SAAS PRINCE SHOULD CONDUCT HIMSELF TO GAIN RENOWN
- XXII. CONCERNING THE EXECUTIVES OF SAAS PRINCES
- XXIII. HOW TO AVOID FLATTERERS AND DECEPTIVE METRICS
- XXIV. WHY CERTAIN SAAS PRINCES HAVE LOST THEIR DOMINIONS

XXV. WHAT FORTUNE CAN EFFECT IN SAAS AFFAIRS AND HOW TO WITHSTAND HER
XXVI. AN EXHORTATION TO GRASP THE CURRENT OPPORTUNITY TO INNOVATE AND LEAD IN THIS NEW ERA OF ARTIFICIAL INTELLIGENCE

CHAPTER I. OF THE VARIOUS KINDS OF SOFTWARE EMPIRES AND THE MEANS BY WHICH THEY ARE ACQUIRED

All states and dominions which hold sway over men are either Software Republics or Principalities. In our modern age, we speak not of hereditary principalities, but of Bootstrapped Startups and Venture-Backed Empires.

Bootstrapped Startups are those which have been sustained by their own revenues from the first line of code, often guided by a single visionary founder or a small council of co-founders. These are more easily held once acquired, for the princes of such domains are accustomed to frugality and know intimately the workings of their realm.

Venture-Backed Empires, on the other hand, are won through the gold of external powers. These grow swiftly, fueled by the ambitions of many stakeholders, but can be more tumultuous to govern. The prince of such a domain must satisfy not only his users but also the lords of Sand Hill Road who have staked their fortunes on his success.

There are also Hybrid Regimes, which begin as Bootstrapped Startups but later take on the characteristics of Venture-Backed Empires. These can be most formidable, for they combine the lean efficiency of the former with the expansionist capabilities of the latter.

In all cases, the difficulty of maintaining power varies directly with the novelty of the prince's acquisition. A wholly new product in an untapped market, like a new prince in a new principality, faces the greatest challenges. For innovation, while glorified, is also feared, and the prince must overcome the skepticism of potential users who cling to their familiar, if inferior, solutions.

Conversely, he who disrupts an existing market must contend with entrenched competitors, much as a usurper must guard against the loyalists of the deposed regime. Yet, if victorious, his position may prove more secure, for users who have actively chosen to switch allegiance often become the most fervent evangelists.

The wise founder, therefore, must consider not only the nature of the market he wishes to conquer but also the means by which he intends to do so. For the path chosen at the outset will shape the challenges and opportunities that lie ahead in the conquest of the digital realm.

CHAPTER II. CONCERNING HEREDITARY SAAS MONARCHIES

I will leave out all discussion of entirely new SaaS products, and instead focus on those that have already achieved Product-Market Fit and now seek to maintain their dominance. I say, then, that in hereditary SaaS states, accustomed to the bloodline of their prince, there are far fewer difficulties in maintaining them than in new ones. For it is sufficient only not to neglect the institutions established by one's predecessors, and then to adapt to market forces as they arise. In this manner, a prince of ordinary industry will always maintain himself in his state, unless some extraordinary and excessive force deprive him of it.

Indeed, the natural subscription model of SaaS businesses provides a form of hereditary revenue that, properly managed, can sustain a product through multiple generations of technology. The prince of such a state has less cause and less necessity to offend his customers; hence it happens that he will be more loved. And unless extraordinary vices cause him to be hated, it is reasonable to expect that his users will be naturally well disposed towards him.

In the succession of SaaS products, antiquity and continuity of user data are powerful forces. One change always leaves the toothing for another. But when you update a long-standing product, the new features can rely upon the old, and thus maintain cohesion in the state, whereas introducing an entirely new system disrupts all foundations and weakens the whole.

Consider the great SaaS empires of our time - the Salesforces, the Slacks, the Zooms. Their longevity is due not to radical reinvention, but to gradual evolution that respects the habits and data of their users. They have mastered the art of introducing novelty without alienation, of progress without disruption.

However, let not the prince of an established SaaS domain grow complacent. For while hereditary states are accustomed to changes in leadership - be it CEOs or product managers - they are utterly intolerant of changes in custom. The prince who introduces a new feature that conflicts with long-standing workflows does so at his peril. It is easier by far to win new customers to a novel interface than to change the habits of those long accustomed to their ways.

Therefore, the prudent maintainer of a SaaS hereditary state will strive always to enhance, never to replace. He will add features judiciously, expand integrations cautiously, and above all, preserve the core experience that won him his throne. For in the realm of software, it is not innovation alone that secures a prince's position, but the delicate balance of progress and familiarity.

CHAPTER III. CONCERNING MIXED SAAS EMPIRES

The greatest test of a SaaS prince's virtue comes not in maintaining their hereditary state, but in the assimilation of new acquisitions. Here lie the seeds of both empire and ruin.

Consider Salesforce, the CRM titan. In its conquest of Slack, it faced the classic dilemma of the mixed empire. Slack's users, accustomed to their swift and simple interface, feared the bloat of their new Salesforce overlords. Meanwhile, Salesforce's veterans eyed the newcomer with suspicion, seeing a potential usurper to their established order.

The difficulties of such conquests arise from an immutable law of human nature: users crave change until it arrives at their doorstep. They rally behind the banner of "disruption" until their own workflows are disrupted. Then, they long for the tyrant they knew.

Microsoft, in its acquisition of GitHub, demonstrated the cunning required of a SaaS prince in mixed domains. They left GitHub's culture largely intact, allowing it to operate as a semi-independent state within their empire. This strategy pacified the open-source zealots who might have revolted against direct Microsoft rule.

For these reasons, Larry Ellison, King of Databases, erred gravely in Oracle's hostile takeover of PeopleSoft. His aggressive assimilation strategy turned PeopleSoft's customer base into a hotbed of rebellion, ripe for exploitation by rival powers like Workday.

The SaaS prince who would conquer and hold mixed empires should heed these maxims:

1. Swift integration is key, but it must be done with a velvet glove, not an iron fist. The wise prince first unites the underlying systems, leaving the familiar facade untouched, lest the users revolt against sudden change.
2. The APIs and data structures of the conquered product are its holy relics. Preserve them, lest you incite a user rebellion.
3. Establish a permanent presence in your new territory. Zoom's acquisition of Keybase failed partly because Zoom's leaders treated it as a distant colony rather than an integral part of their empire.
4. Beware the strength of third-party integrations in your new domain. They can become shadow governments, siphoning away the loyalty of your users. Observe how Salesforce, in its wisdom, maintained Slack's integrations with Google Workspace and Microsoft Teams, even as these served rival powers. By doing so, they prevented a mass exodus of users who relied on these connections.
5. The prince must move his most trusted nobles into key positions within the conquered territory, that they might instill the virtues of his realm without extinguishing the native customs that made the acquisition desirable. Thus did Amazon with Twitch, preserving the appearance of independence while

ensuring true power rested with those loyal to the crown.

The prince who neglects these principles will find their newly acquired users slipping through their fingers like sand. They will be left with nothing but a costly tech stack and a cautionary tale for the next generation of SaaS conquerors.

The wise prince must also be wary of the serpents within his own court when acquiring new territories. Consider the folly of IBM, a once-mighty empire, in their conquest of the Rational kingdom. Rational had itself annexed the small but innovative realm of Neuvis. Yet, within IBM's sprawling dominion, a jealous noble whispered poison into the ear of the prince. This noble, fearing the strength of Neuvis would diminish his own standing, persuaded the prince to lay waste to the newly acquired territory, allowing his own inferior product to reign unchallenged. But lo, in protecting the noble's pride, IBM lost the very advantage they sought to gain. The internal product floundered, and the acquisition became naught but a costly lesson.

This tale teaches us that a prince must balance the loyalties of his court with the potential of his conquests. To destroy a newly acquired asset for the sake of internal politics is to poison one's own well. A truly cunning prince would find a way to integrate the new strength without alienating his nobles, perhaps by giving them stake in its success or demonstrating how it complements rather than threatens their positions.

Observe how Intuit, in its conquest of Mailchimp, seeks to expand its small business empire without smothering the very innovation that made Mailchimp attractive. This is the high art of the mixed SaaS empire - to expand one's domain while nurturing the unique strengths that made the acquisition valuable in the first place.

CHAPTER IV. WHY CERTAIN SAAS ACQUISITIONS DO NOT REBEL AGAINST THEIR NEW OVERLORDS

Consider the dominion of Atlassian, and how after its conquest of Trello, the vanquished product did not rebel against its new master, even when the founders departed. This stands in stark contrast to the acquisition of Sunrise by Microsoft, where the calendar app, once beloved, withered and died under its new reign.

The difference lies in the nature of these SaaS principalities before their conquest. There are two types of digital realms difficult to hold upon acquisition: One, where the product is singular in purpose but fiercely loved, its users united in devotion. The other, where the product serves as a platform, hosting a multitude of third-party integrations and customizations.

Trello, in the first case, was a realm of the second type. Its power was distributed among many Powerups and integrations, each serving a specific need. When Atlassian conquered this land, they did not need to extinguish these local powers, but merely to ensure their loyalty. The users, accustomed to this feudal structure, found little changed in their daily workflows and thus had no cause for rebellion.

Sunrise, however, was a realm of the first type, a principality unified by the vision of its founding prince. Its strength lay not in vassals or fiefdoms, but in the unwaivering devotion of its subjects to a singular, divine interface. When the Microsoftian Empire seized this land, they sought not to rule it, but to strip it for parts, to absorb its essence into their sprawling Outlook dominion. In their haste to consolidate power, they shattered the covenant between Sunrise and its adherents. The users, finding their cherished customs trampled and their familiar rituals disrupted, saw no choice but to seek new lands. Thus, a conquest that should have strengthened the empire instead scattered its newly acquired subjects to rival territories.

The prince must understand: when acquiring a product with a unified, devoted user base, it is folly to immediately assimilate it. Instead, one must govern it as a semi-autonomous region, gradually aligning it with the larger empire over time. This is the wisdom Salesforce displayed in their conquest of Slack.

Conversely, when acquiring a platform-like product, the prince must focus on winning the loyalty of the ecosystem it supports. Adobe, in its acquisition of Behance, understood this principle well. They did not seek to fold Behance immediately into their Creative Cloud, but instead nurtured its community and integrations, understanding that the power of Behance lay in its network, not merely its features.

Let it be known that in SaaS empires, as in the kingdoms of old, it is easier to hold a conquered territory accustomed to living under the rule of others, so long as the local customs are respected. But when acquiring a product that has known only the rule of its founders, the prince must take great care not to upset the delicate balance that has bred such fierce loyalty.

The cunning prince, therefore, must tailor his approach to the nature of his conquest. He must know when to assimilate and when to accommodate, when to impose his will and when to bow to local customs. For in the realm of SaaS, the users are fickle subjects, ever ready to migrate to greener pastures should their needs be neglected.

CHAPTER V. HOW TO GOVERN SAAS FIEFDOMS THAT, PRIOR TO ACQUISITION, LIVED UNDER THEIR OWN LAWS

When a prince acquires a new SaaS realm that differs from his hereditary state - as when a product-led growth company conquers a sales-driven fiefdom, or when a waterfall development duchy annexes an agile principality - he will find it most challenging to hold them steady. This difficulty arises not from a lack of might or cunning, but from the very nature of these conquered lands and their customs.

To maintain dominion over such acquisitions, one of three methods must be employed:

The first, most brutal, and least advisable in our enlightened age of "user-centric design" and "employee satisfaction," is to lay waste to their existing culture. To raze their customs to the ground, salt the earth of their prior methodologies, and rebuild in the image of the conquering company. This was the approach of Oracle in its conquest of PeopleSoft, where they put the entire court of PeopleSoft to the sword, replacing them with Oracle's own nobles. While effective in the short term, it breeds resentment and often destroys the very value the prince sought to acquire.

The second method is for the prince to take up residence in the new territory, establishing his court within their walls. This was the path chosen by Facebook in its acquisition of Instagram. By allowing Instagram to maintain its own castle in San Francisco, separate from the Facebook stronghold in Menlo Park, Mark Zuckerberg could keep a watchful eye on his new subjects while allowing them to maintain the illusion of autonomy. This method is costly and requires constant vigilance, but can be effective in gradually assimilating a prized conquest.

The third method, most suited to the cunning prince, is to allow them to live under their own laws, drawing tribute in the form of revenue and data, while installing a puppet government loyal to your cause. Google, in its wisdom, employed this strategy with YouTube. They allowed YouTube to maintain its own culture and operations, while ensuring that key decisions aligned with Google's grand strategy. This method is least likely to breed discontent, but requires a deft hand to maintain the balance of power.

It must be noted that SaaS realms accustomed to operating independently are most easily held if they have not tasted the nectar of acquisition before. Virgin territories, like Figma before Adobe's conquest, are more pliable than those who have already cast off one corporate overlord, like Flickr in its tumultuous history.

The prudent prince must also consider the nature of his new subjects. Engineers, those fickle wizards of the digital realm, are quick to flee if their arcane practices are disrupted. Product managers and designers, the nobility of the SaaS world, must be courted and their loyalty secured, lest they foment rebellion or lead an exodus to rival lands.

In all matters of conquest, the prince must weigh the swift consolidation of power against the perils of inciting revolt. For in these digital realms, where subjects may transfer their loyalties with but a gesture, the art of governance is akin to grasping at mist. A wise prince knows the folly of ruling over a wasteland of abandoned code and fleeing vassals. Far better to preside over a thriving, semi-autonomous province, extracting tribute and allegiance through subtle manipulations, than to find oneself master of a deserted digital citadel. For power in the SaaS kingdoms is not measured in lines of code or server farms, but in the fickle hearts and minds of users who may, at any moment, pledge fealty to a rival throne.

CHAPTER VI. CONCERNING NEW SAAS PRINCIPALITIES ACQUIRED THROUGH ONE'S OWN INNOVATION AND FORTITUDE

Let us now turn our gaze to those audacious princes who, through their own innovation and fortitude, carve out new dominions in the vast digital wilderness. These are the founders and product visionaries who, like Romulus of old, draw a line in the sand and declare, "Here shall rise a new empire."

Such endeavors are at once the most glorious and the most perilous. For in founding a new SaaS realm, the prince cannot rely on inherited loyalty or established customs. Every user must be won, every feature forged from raw code. The difficulties are manifold, for all innovators have as their enemies those who prospered under the old order, and lukewarm defenders in those who may prosper under the new.

Consider the realm of Slack, founded by the visionary Stewart Butterfield. When he sought to overthrow the tyranny of email, he faced not only the entrenched powers of Microsoft and Google but also the inertia of a million corporate serfs accustomed to their Outlook chains. Yet through superior design and viral adoption strategies, he carved out a mighty empire.

The prince who would found a new SaaS domain must possess not only technical prowess but also the cunning of a fox and the strength of a lion. He must be prepared to pivot swiftly, as young Mark Zuckerberg did when he transformed the modest principality of Facebook from a collegiate dalliance into a global superpower.

However, let it be known that those who rise from obscurity to digital nobility through fortune and foreign aid alone seldom maintain their position. The annals of startup history are littered with the bones of princes who, flush with venture capital, built mighty castles on foundations of sand. They rise quickly, but are cast down at the first winter storm of market corrections.

But those who rely mainly on their own prowess and innovation, like the houses of Bezos and Musk, have a firmer foundation. The difficulty lies in laying new modes and orders. For the founder must be both architect and governor, drawing up constitutions of code and forging alliances in the byzantine world of APIs and integrations.

The wise prince, in launching his SaaS kingdom, must also be prepared to stand alone. In the earliest days, when the product is but a shadow of its potential, he will find few true allies. The masses, ever skeptical of the new, will mock his vision as folly. Rival princes will dismiss him as a pretender. Even his own court may whisper doubts.

In these trying times, the prince must be as steadfast as Salesforce's Benioff, who held firm to his vision of cloud-based CRM when the world still clung to on-premise solutions. He must be as adaptable as Netflix's Hastings, who cannibalized his own DVD realm to establish dominance in the streaming lands.

Let it be understood that in founding a new SaaS principality, half depends on prowess, half on fortune. But prowess must prevail, for fortune is a fickle mistress, especially in the tempestuous seas of technology. The prince who relies too heavily on the winds of market trends may soon find himself dashed upon the rocks of obsolescence.

Thus, to the ambitious SaaS visionary, I say: Steel yourself for hardship, for the path of innovation is treacherous. But know that should you succeed, should your code take root and flourish, you will have built not just a company, but a legacy. Your name will be etched in the annals of tech history, your methods studied by aspiring princes for generations to come.

For there is no more certain path to digital immortality than to disrupt the old order and forge a new world from the molten silicon of innovation.

CHAPTER VII. CONCERNING SAAS PRINCIPALITIES ACQUIRED BY FORTUNE OR THE FAVOR OF THE MASSES

Let us now turn our attention to those SaaS princes who rise not through their own genius alone, but are elevated by the capricious winds of fortune or the sudden adoration of the digital masses. These are realms born not of careful planning, but of serendipity and the fickle favor of the market.

Such principalities are gained with little effort, but maintained with great difficulty. Like Icarus, these princes are lifted high on borrowed wings, but the sun of sustainable growth may yet melt their waxen fortitude.

Consider the realm of Clubhouse, which rose to prominence as swiftly as the morning mist. In the time of the great plague, when the masses were sequestered in their homes, this audio kingdom offered a balm for their isolation. Princes and peasants alike flocked to its digital halls, and for a brief, shining moment, it seemed a new power had emerged in the social media lands.

But lo, how quickly the tides of fortune can turn! As the plague receded and the established powers of Twitter and Facebook erected their own audio bastions, Clubhouse found itself adrift. The prince who rises to power on such tempestuous seas must quickly learn to navigate, lest he be dashed upon the rocks of irrelevance.

Or ponder the fate of Pokémon Go, a realm that burst forth like a supernova, engulfing the world in augmented reality fervor. Niantic, its progenitor, found itself suddenly master of a vast digital empire, its subjects roaming the physical world in pursuit of virtual creatures. Yet, as swiftly as it rose, its population dwindled, leaving behind a diminished yet stable duchy where once stood a global phenomenon.

The prince who finds himself thrust into power by such means faces a precarious position. Like Cesare Borgia, elevated by his father's influence, these SaaS rulers must quickly establish their own foundations lest their empire crumble when fortune's favor wanes.

To maintain such a principality, the prince must swiftly transition from fortunate fool to cunning strategist. He must, like the founders of Instagram, recognize the fleeting nature of viral fame and seek the protection of a greater power - in their case, the sprawling Facebook empire.

Alternatively, the prince might follow the path of Zoom, which found itself thrust into prominence by the great plague. Its rulers, rather than bask in their newfound glory, used this fortune to rapidly fortify their defenses, expand their features, and entrench themselves in the workflows of their subjects. Thus, what began as a fortunate accident of timing became a formidable and lasting empire.

The wise prince, elevated by fortune, must also guard against the complacency that easy success breeds. Many are the founders who, intoxicated by early adulation, neglected to build the sturdy foundations necessary for lasting dominion. They are like those who build castles upon sand, impressive to behold but quick to fall when the tide turns.

Let it be known that principalities gained by fortune are like saplings in a storm - they may grow quickly, but their roots are shallow. The prince who would transform such a fortunate accident into a lasting dynasty must act decisively. He must use the window granted by fortune to build real value, to entrench his product so deeply in the lives of his users that they cannot imagine a world without it.

For in the realm of SaaS, as in the kingdoms of old, fortune may grant power, but only wisdom and cunning can maintain it. The masses are fickle, their attention easily swayed by the next digital bauble. The prince who relies solely on their fleeting adoration will soon find himself ruler of an empty domain, his once-bustling servers echoing with the ghosts of abandoned user accounts.

Thus, to the SaaS prince blessed by fortune, I say: Be grateful for your luck, but do not trust in its constancy. Use the opportunity granted to forge a true empire, one built not on the shifting sands of viral trends, but on the bedrock of user value and technical excellence. For only then can you hope to transform your moment of glory into a lasting digital legacy.

CHAPTER VIII. CONCERNING THOSE WHO HAVE OBTAINED SAAS DOMINION BY NEFARIOUS MEANS

It may be considered a matter of infamy to discuss the darker arts of SaaS empire-building, yet a true examination of power must not shy away from the shadows. For in the digital realm, as in the principalities of old, there are those who ascend not through virtue or fortune alone, but through cunning, deceit, and a willingness to transgress the boundaries of ethical conduct.

Consider the realm of Uber, whose rise to power was marked by a flagrant disregard for the laws of the lands it sought to conquer. Its founder, Travis Kalanick, like Agathocles of Syracuse, did not blanch at the thought of upending entire industries and flouting local ordinances. With each city it entered, Uber left a wake of disrupted markets and outraged regulators. Yet, for a time, its growth seemed unstoppable, its valuation soaring to dizzying heights.

Or ponder the case of Theranos, whose princess, Elizabeth Holmes, wove a tapestry of lies so grand it ensnared even the wisest of investors. Like Oliverotto da Fermo, who rose to power through treachery, Holmes built her blood-testing empire on foundations of sand and secrets. For a brief, shining moment, she was hailed as a visionary, her company valued at billions. But as with all such ill-gotten gains, the reckoning was swift and merciless when the truth was laid bare.

It must be noted that such methods, while potentially effective in the short term, rarely lead to lasting dynasties. The prince who rises through deceit finds himself forever watching his back, his energies consumed by maintaining the elaborate facades that shield his misdeeds from scrutiny.

Yet, it would be folly to claim that no enduring empire has been built on ethically questionable grounds. Facebook, that behemoth of the social media lands, has weathered storms of controversy regarding its data practices and impact on democratic institutions. Its prince, Zuckerberg, has shown a remarkable ability to navigate these treacherous waters, offering apologies and promises of reform while continuing to expand his dominion.

The aspiring SaaS prince must weigh carefully the allure of such methods. For while they may offer swift gains, they also court swift retribution. The modern digital age, with its interconnected networks of information, makes it increasingly difficult to hide one's misdeeds. A single whistleblower, a leaked document, or an ill-timed data breach can bring even the mightiest empire to its knees.

Moreover, the subjects of SaaS realms – be they users, customers, or employees – have grown wise to the ways of unscrupulous rulers. They are quick to revolt, to abandon platforms that betray their trust, and to rally behind competitors who promise more ethical governance.

Yet, let us not be naive. In the cutthroat world of SaaS, where fortunes are made and lost in the blink of an eye, there will always be those who are willing to skirt the edges of propriety in pursuit of power. The wise prince must be aware of these darker arts, not to practice them, but to guard against them.

For those who do choose this perilous path, let them heed this warning: If wickedness must be employed, let it be done swiftly and decisively, and then immediately followed by acts of apparent virtue and user benefit. For the masses have short memories, and a prince who can quickly transition from necessary evil to benevolent ruler may yet salvage his reign.

In the end, the SaaS prince must decide whether the fleeting glory of ill-gotten gains is worth the constant paranoia, the threat of swift downfall, and the indelible stain upon one's legacy. For while history may forgive a multitude of sins in the face of lasting success, the digital realm is far less forgiving. In this age of instant communication and eternal digital records, the wicked prince may find that his misdeeds outlive his empire, echoing through the annals of cautionary tech tales long after his product has faded into obsolescence.

CHAPTER IX. CONCERNING THE CIVIL SAAS PRINCIPALITY

Let us now turn our gaze to those SaaS principalities that rise not in the untamed wilderness of new markets, but within the bustling cities of established digital domains. These are the realms carved out amidst fierce competition, where users are not virgin territory to be claimed, but citizens to be wooed from rival princes.

In such civil principalities, power is gained not through conquest alone, but through the art of factions. For in every market, there are those users dissatisfied with the current order, yearning for a new prince to address their neglected needs. The wise SaaS ruler must identify these factions and rally them to his banner.

Consider the ascension of Slack in the lands of business communication. It did not invent a new form of discourse, but rather identified the discontented masses laboring under the tyranny of email and clumsy project management tools. By appealing to these users' desires for swifter, more informal communication, Slack carved out a mighty principality in a realm once thought fully claimed.

Or ponder the rise of Zoom in the video conferencing kingdoms. WebEx and Skype had long ruled these lands, but they grew complacent, their interfaces cluttered and cumbersome. Zoom, perceiving the frustration of the common user, offered a simpler path to virtual assembly. In doing so, they turned the very simplicity scorned by established powers into a rallying cry for a new order.

The prince who would establish dominion in such contested territories must master the delicate balance of innovation and familiarity. Push too far into novel territory, and users will balk at the learning curve. Cleave too closely to established norms, and you offer no compelling reason for migration. The art lies in presenting a vision of the future that feels both fresh and intuitive.

Moreover, the civil SaaS prince must be a master of illusion. For users are fickle creatures, easily swayed by the appearance of momentum. A product that seems ascendant will draw curious onlookers, who in turn make it truly ascendant. Thus, the clever prince must create the impression of inevitable victory, even in the early stages of his campaign.

Yet, let the aspiring ruler be warned: in civil principalities, the very factions that elevate you to power can just as swiftly cast you down. Today's revolutionary feature is tomorrow's outdated paradigm. The users who flocked to your banner seeking change may grow restless if that change is not continuously delivered.

In such realms, the prince must also guard against the twin dangers of overreach and stagnation. Expand your feature set too rapidly, and you risk becoming the very bloated behemoth you once rallied against. Innovate too slowly, and hungry upstarts will woo away your user base with promises of a brighter tomorrow.

The wise prince in a civil SaaS principality must also master the art of coexistence. Unlike in new markets where one might reign supreme, established domains often support multiple powers. Your victory need not come through the total annihilation of your rivals, but through the careful cultivation of your niche. Indeed, the presence of competitors can be a boon, validating your market and providing a foil against which to define your unique value.

Let us examine the strategy of Notion in the realm of productivity tools. Rather than seeking to overthrow Google or Microsoft entirely, they positioned themselves as a unifying force, a bridge between disparate tools. By doing so, they carved out a principality that coexists with larger powers while steadily expanding its borders.

In all matters of civil SaaS governance, the prince must remember that power ultimately flows from the will of the users. Unlike in hereditary principalities where habit and tradition hold sway, or in new conquests where novelty alone might suffice, the civil SaaS prince rules by continuous consent. Each login, each renewed subscription, is a referendum on your right to rule.

Thus, to the SaaS prince aspiring to power in established markets, I say: Be bold in your vision but measured in your execution. Court the dissatisfied but do not neglect the contented. Create the illusion of inevitability while remaining adaptable to shifting tides. For in the civil SaaS principality, power is not seized in a single, glorious campaign, but earned through countless small victories in the hearts and workflows of your users.

CHAPTER X. CONCERNING THE WAY IN WHICH THE STRENGTH OF A SAAS PRINCIPALITY SHOULD BE MEASURED

In the assessment of SaaS dominions, one must look beyond the glittering facades of user interfaces and the siren songs of growth metrics. For as the strength of a fortress lies not in the height of its walls but in the depth of its foundations, so too must we plumb the depths of a SaaS realm to truly gauge its might.

First, let us speak of the prince who can defend his digital lands through his own power, without resorting to mercenary developers or the fickle allegiance of venture capitalists. Such a prince, whose coffers overflow with recurring revenue, whose armies of loyal users march forth to spread his gospel, stands upon the firmest of grounds. He need not fear the capricious winds of market sentiment, for his realm is self-sustaining.

Consider the duchy of Basecamp, whose princes, DHH and Fried, have long scorned the siren call of external gold. Their compact yet formidable realm draws strength not from the size of its population, but from the fervor of its adherents. Like a city-state of old, it stands proud and independent amidst sprawling empires.

Yet, let us not be deceived by the allure of independence alone. For there are SaaS kingdoms of such vast expanse and complexity that they cannot be ruled by a single prince, however capable. These are the realms that must be garrisoned by armies of specialists - from the wizards of infrastructure to the alchemists of user experience.

In judging such expansive dominions, one must look to the loyalty of these garrisons. Are they mercenaries, ready to flee at the first sign of winter? Or are they true believers, bound to the realm by chains of equity and vision? The prince whose lieutenants' fortunes rise and fall with his own can sleep more soundly than he whose court is filled with guns for hire.

Examine closely the vassals of these SaaS kingdoms - those third-party integrations and partnerships that extend the realm's influence. A principality buttressed by a thriving ecosystem of allied powers is far stronger than one which stands alone. Yet beware the vassal that grows too powerful, for today's ally may be tomorrow's usurper.

In this age of cloud and distributed systems, the wise observer must also consider the geography of a SaaS realm. Is it bound to a single land, vulnerable to the whims of local potentates? Or has it spread its essence across many domains, resilient against the failure of any single region? The prince whose realm spans the globe need fear no local tyrant.

Let us not neglect the oft-overlooked strength that lies in the arcane scrolls of documentation and the sacred rites of onboarding. For what good is a mighty fortress if none can find the gate? The SaaS prince who arms his users with knowledge builds an army far more formidable than he who hoards secrets.

Peer deeply into the catacombs of technical debt, for therein lies a poison that can fell even the mightiest of empires. A gleaming palace built atop a foundation of hastily cobbled code is a realm living on borrowed time. The truly strong SaaS principality is one whose inner workings are as elegant as its outer appearance.

Finally, measure the adaptability of the realm. In these times of perpetual change, the capacity to pivot is as crucial as the ability to stand firm. The prince who can swiftly redeploy his forces to meet new threats or seize new opportunities possesses a strength beyond mere numbers or riches.

Thus, to those who would gauge the true might of a SaaS principality, I say: Look not to the vanity metrics trumpeted by town criers, nor to the hollow boasts of self-proclaimed unicorns. Instead, examine the foundations, test the loyalty of its people, survey its allies, probe its resilience, and measure its capacity for change. For in the ever-shifting landscape of the digital realms, true strength lies not in momentary glory, but in the capacity to endure and evolve.

CHAPTER XI. CONCERNING OPEN SOURCE PRINCIPALITIES

Let us now turn our gaze to those curious dominions known as Open Source Principalities, which stand apart from the common run of SaaS realms. These are lands governed not by the iron will of a single prince, but by the collective wisdom of their contributors. They are at once everywhere and nowhere, their borders as porous as mist, their riches freely given to all who would partake.

These principalities, like the ecclesiastical states of old, are maintained by powers which reason cannot fully explain, and are created by exalted means which the mind of man cannot fathom. For they are sustained and exalted by the divine hand of Collaboration, fortified by the holy writ of Licenses, and spread by the evangelism of passionate disciples.

Consider the realm of Linux, that vast and sprawling empire that underpins countless digital kingdoms. Its strength lies not in armies or gold, but in the fervent belief of its adherents. Princes of the mightiest tech realms bow before its altars, even as they wage war amongst themselves. It is a power that grows not by conquest, but by conversion.

Or ponder the curious case of MySQL, a principality that found itself absorbed into the Oracle empire, yet whose essence remained free, forking into the MariaDB realm. Here we see the unique resilience of these open dominions – even when their physical assets are seized, their spirit can take flight, reconstituting elsewhere.

The prince who seeks to understand these lands must abandon many of the maxims that govern traditional SaaS warfare. For here, wealth is measured not in gold, but in contributions. Power flows not from the top down, but bubbles up from a myriad of sources. The leader of such a realm is less a prince than a steward, guiding rather than commanding.

Yet, let not the aspiring SaaS ruler dismiss these principalities as toothless utopias. For within their seemingly chaotic structure lies a power that can topple empires. Witness how the Kubernetes covenant, born from the halls of Google, now holds sway over the very infrastructure of the cloud, bending even the mightiest providers to its will.

Indeed, the wise SaaS prince may find great advantage in aligning himself with these open realms. By contributing to their cause, he may earn goodwill and influence far beyond his own borders. By building upon their foundations, he may erect mighty edifices without the burden of laying every stone himself.

However, the prince must tread carefully in these lands. The denizens of open source principalities are quick to anger at any sign of exploitation. Many a corporate prince has seen his reputation tarnished by clumsy attempts to exert control over these free domains.

For those SaaS rulers who would engage with these principalities, here are the commandments you must observe:

1. Thou shalt contribute back to the community, lest ye be seen as a parasite.

2. Thou shalt respect the sacred licenses, for they are the constitution of these lands.
3. Thou shalt not attempt to seize control, but rather guide through merit and contribution.
4. Thou shalt be transparent in thy dealings, for secrecy is anathema in these realms.
5. Thou shalt honor the meritocracy, elevating those who contribute regardless of their origin.

The prince who masters the art of coexistence with these open source principalities gains access to a wellspring of innovation and goodwill. Yet he who seeks to exploit them may find himself cast out, his name a curse upon the lips of developers.

In truth, these open source dominions represent a power both ancient and new. They harken back to the commons of old, yet thrive in the digital age. They are the monasteries of our time, preserving and advancing knowledge for the benefit of all.

Thus, to the SaaS prince, I say: Ignore these realms at your peril, for they shape the very bedrock upon which your empire stands. Engage with them wisely, and you may find allies more steadfast than any mercenary army. For in the ever-shifting sands of the digital world, the open source principalities stand as beacons of stability and innovation, their influence reaching far beyond their apparent borders.

CHAPTER XII. CONCERNING THE VARIOUS KINDS OF DEVELOPMENT FORCES AND OUTSOURCED MERCENARIES

Having discoursed particularly on the chief qualities of SaaS principalities, and having considered in some degree the causes of their being good or bad, it now remains for us to discuss the means of offense and defense which a prince may employ in these digital realms. We have seen that a wise prince must lay solid foundations, for without them, all else is but shifting sand. And what are these foundations if not the armies that build and maintain the prince's digital dominion?

Let it be known that the armies which defend and expand a SaaS principality are of three kinds: the prince's own forces, outsourced mercenaries, and auxiliary troops. The prince's own forces are those developers, designers, and engineers who swear fealty directly to the realm, bound by oaths of equity and vision. Outsourced mercenaries are those hired guns, contracted for specific battles or campaigns. Auxiliary troops are those borrowed from allied powers, often in the form of vendor partnerships or platform dependencies.

A prince who founds his state on mercenaries alone will never be stable or secure. For mercenaries are disunited, thirsty for power, undisciplined, and disloyal. They are brave among friends and cowards before enemies. They have no fear of God and keep no faith with men. Ruin is deferred only as long as attack is deferred. In peace, you are despoiled by them; in war, by the enemy.

Consider the fate of Quibi, that ill-fated principality which relied heavily on Hollywood mercenaries to create its content. Though these hired guns were skilled in their crafts, they lacked the true devotion to the realm's vision. When the tides of war turned against Quibi, these mercenaries were quick to abandon ship, leaving the principality to crumble.

The wise prince, therefore, has always avoided these outsourced troops and relied on his own. He would rather lose with his own men than win with outsiders, for he judges that a victory won with the arms of others is no true victory. Look to the realm of Basecamp, where the princes DHH and Fried have long eschewed the siren call of venture capital and outsourced development, preferring instead to build their forces slowly and steadily with those who truly believe in their cause.

Yet, let us not be hasty in our dismissal of all forms of auxiliary forces. For in these complex times, no principality can stand entirely alone. The art lies in knowing how to employ these external powers without becoming dependent upon them. Witness how the Shopify empire has grown mighty by providing a platform for merchant vassals, empowering them while maintaining ultimate control.

For the prince who must expand rapidly, a mix of forces may be employed, but with great caution. If mercenaries must be engaged, let them be surrounded by loyal troops, their work scrutinized and integrated by those who hold true fealty to the realm. And let these contracts be short, lest the mercenaries begin to see themselves as indispensable.

CHAPTER XIV. THAT WHICH CONCERNS A SAAS PRINCE ON THE SUBJECT OF THE ART OF PRODUCT DEVELOPMENT

A prince ought to have no other aim or thought, nor select anything else for his study, than the art of product development and its rules; for this is the sole art that belongs to him who rules. It is of such great import that it not only upholds those born with SaaS crowns but often enables founders to rise from obscure startups to great empires. Conversely, we see that when princes have devoted more thought to delicate features than to code and architecture, they have lost their thrones.

The first cause of a SaaS prince losing his state is neglect of this art; the first cause of winning a state is proficiency in it. Our Francesco Salesforce, along with many others, from mere startup founders became mighty emperors by cultivating this art alone. And the lack of it lost Blockbuster its empire, when faced with the technological onslaught of Netflix.

A wise prince, therefore, ought never to idle in times of peace, but should diligently explore new technological frontiers, that he may effectively wield them in times of market turbulence, and thus be prepared to withstand the blows of fickle user demands.

To exercise the intellect of the prince, he ought to study customer behavior, immerse himself in analytics, and examine the release cycles of antiquity. He should observe how the great SaaS leaders of yore positioned their

Native technologies are those which spring from a prince's own developers, grounded in his own vision and needs. These are the only true and faithful technologies, the only genuine source of a realm's strength. All other forms are either corrupt or open to corruption by the ambitions of their true masters.

Thus, let no prince who wishes to maintain his state stake his future on auxiliary or mixed technologies. Let him instead invest in native innovation, cultivating a core of technological strength that is truly his own. For it is upon this foundation that lasting SaaS empires are built, able to weather the storms of market shifts and technological revolutions alike.

forces, they too are of limited value. For in times of triumph, it is unclear whether the victory belongs to the native or the auxiliary technologies, and in defeat, they compound one's losses.

The valorous prince relies chiefly on his own arms and native technologies. For there is no comparison between a prince who stands alone in his technological prowess, and one who depends on the charity of external powers.

Let us examine the realm of Epic Games, a principality of considerable native strength. From the foundry of their own genius, they forged the Unreal Engine, a weapon of such power and versatility that it has become the very bedrock of their empire. This native technology has granted Epic not just the means to craft their own legendary sagas like Fortnite, but also the power to arm countless other realms in exchange for tribute.

It is upon this foundation of native strength that Epic now dares to challenge the very powers upon whose platforms it once depended. In contesting Apple's dominion over its App Store, Epic demonstrates that a prince with true native technology can rise to threaten even the mightiest of overlords. The wise prince observes this conflict closely, for it portends a shifting of the very foundations upon which many SaaS realms are built.

I conclude, therefore, that without native technologies, no principality is secure; nay, it is wholly dependent on fortune, lacking the strength to defend itself in adversity. And it has always been the opinion of wise princes that nothing is so weak and unstable as a technological dominion not founded on native innovation.

CHAPTER XIII. CONCERNING AUXILIARY, MIXED, AND NATIVE TECHNOLOGIES

Auxiliary technologies are those which a SaaS prince borrows from other powers to bolster his own realm. These may take the form of cloud infrastructures, third-party APIs, or development frameworks. And while they may seem potent and expedient, they are, in truth, most perilous and unreliable.

For he who stands upon auxiliary technologies stands upon nothing, being without valor or discipline of his own. United and resolute they may appear in times of prosperity, but come adversity, they may turn to their own interests, leaving the borrowing prince bereft.

Consider the realm of Parler, which built its fortifications upon the AWS cloud. When strife arose, AWS withdrew its support, and Parler found itself castleless and exposed, its very existence imperiled by the loss of its auxiliary foundation. This tale serves as a stark reminder that even the mightiest of auxiliary powers may prove fickle when political winds shift.

The prudent prince, therefore, will never resort to auxiliary technologies to avoid travail, for in them he will find only ruin. Far better to fail with one's own forces than to succeed with others', for success born of auxiliary strength brings no true glory.

Mixed technologies are those where a prince combines auxiliary powers with his own native solutions. While less immediately dangerous than pure auxiliary

In matters of auxiliary troops – those technologies and platforms upon which a SaaS principality may be built – the prince must tread with even greater care. For while these may offer swift advancement, they also place the fate of the realm in foreign hands. Many a promising principality has found itself at the mercy of platform changes from the likes of Apple or Google.

The wise prince, therefore, seeks a balance. He builds his core forces from those who believe in the realm's mission, supplementing them judiciously with specialized mercenaries when needed. He forms alliances with powerful platforms but always maintains a path of retreat, never entrusting the entire foundation of his realm to forces he does not control.

Let it be known that in the ever-shifting battlefields of the SaaS world, the most valuable army is one that can adapt swiftly to new threats and opportunities. The prince must foster not just loyalty, but continuous learning among his troops. For the developer who remains mired in outdated techniques is no better than a knight who clings to his lance in an age of gunpowder.

In conclusion, to the SaaS prince I say: Build your forces with care, for they are the lifeblood of your realm. Invest in those who will stand with you through both triumph and tribulation. Use mercenaries and auxiliary troops with caution, always remembering that true strength comes from within. For in the end, it is not the size of the army that matters, but its loyalty, skill, and adaptability. These are the qualities that will see your digital dominion through the storms of disruption and the sieges of competition.

products, why certain features triumphed while others faltered, and apply these lessons to his own realm. Let him emulate the methods of release and deployment of those emperors who have excelled most in revamping their products.

It is told of Jeff Bezos that, among other pursuits, he devoted himself to imagining a future of one-click purchases and cloud dominance long before such things were feasible. And so should a SaaS prince act, keeping his engineering skills sharp even as he directs his realm from the throne of product management.

Nor should the prince neglect the practical exercise of product development. In addition to keeping his realm in good order and constant readiness, he ought always to keep his engineers engaged in coding sprints and hackathons. First, to keep their skills honed; and secondly, to familiarize himself with the terrain of his digital realm, understanding which features can be swiftly deployed, where technical debt lurks, and how best to outmaneuver rivals in future product battles.

Moreover, to better comprehend the nature of new territories he may wish to conquer, the prince must become a user of his own product and those of his competitors. For only by experiencing the triumphs and tribulations of the user can he truly know where to direct his forces of innovation.

Princes who have neglected these preparations and focused solely on the luxuries of product roadmaps and market positioning have lost their states. The disdain for this art of product development is the chief cause of ruin for many a SaaS realm. For the gap between a prince versed only in business strategy and one proficient in both strategy and technology is so vast that the former can in no way command respect from his engineers or rely on their loyalty.

Let us consider the cautionary tale of Boeing, a once-mighty empire in the realm of aviation. When they elevated a prince skilled in finance to the throne, eschewing those with deep knowledge of aeronautical engineering, their fortunes took a perilous turn. Under his reign, Boeing's flying fortresses, once revered for their reliability, began to falter and fall from the sky. The prince's focus on financial engineering over aeronautical engineering led to a series of calamities that tarnished the realm's reputation and shook the very foundations of their empire. Though Boeing's dominion lies beyond our SaaS lands, the lesson rings true across all technological realms: a prince who cannot speak the language of his engineers risks building castles in the air, impressive to shareholders but perilous to those who must dwell within them.

A prince who lacks this technical skill lacks the very essence of a tech leader, for it is this which elevates a mere manager to a true visionary. Without it, he will be held in low esteem by his developers, just as ignorance of the user experience will make him despised by his customers. He ought not, therefore, to let a day pass without engaging in both the technical and experiential aspects of his product, as did Steve Jobs in times of peace, who labored more intensely in his product labs than on stages before adoring crowds.

History teaches us that those SaaS princes who have achieved great feats have held coding and architecture in high esteem and have always devoted themselves to it. This was the case with Bill Gates in his ascent, who never let a product cycle pass without leading by example, often diving into the code himself to set the standard for his realm.

Thus, a SaaS prince should not only attend to present product troubles but also prepare for future ones, facing them with all his skill, so that when challenges arise, he will be prepared to meet them. As the sages of agile development teach: sprint not just for the current release, but for the product roadmap that stretches beyond the horizon.

CHAPTER XV. CONCERNING THINGS FOR WHICH SAAS LEADERS AND THEIR PRODUCTS ARE PRAISED OR BLAMED

It remains now to be seen what ought to be the conduct and bearing of a SaaS prince towards his products and his users. I know that many have written on this point, and I expect I shall be considered presumptuous in mentioning it again, especially as in my treatment of it I shall depart from the methods of other discourse. But, it being my intention to write a thing which shall be useful to him who apprehends it, it appears to me more appropriate to follow up the real truth of the matter than the imagination of it.

Many have imagined platforms and products that neither have been known or seen in reality. For how we deploy is so far from how we ought to deploy, that he who neglects what is done for what ought to be done, sooner effects his ruin than his preservation; for a man who wishes to act entirely up to his professions of virtue soon meets with what destroys him among so much that is evil.

Hence it is necessary for a prince wishing to hold his own to know how to do wrong, and to make use of it or not according to necessity. Therefore, putting on one side imaginary things concerning a SaaS leader, and discussing those which are real, I say that all men when they are spoken of, and SaaS princes more than others, are remarkable for some of those qualities which bring them either blame or praise.

Thus, one is reputed generous in freemium offerings, another miserly in data limits; one is reputed agile, another rigid; one privacy-focused, another data-hungry; one user-centric, another revenue-driven; one innovative, another derivative; one open-source advocate, another proprietary guardian; one scalable, another niche; one hands-on, another delegator.

I know that every one will confess that it would be most praiseworthy in a SaaS prince to exhibit all the above qualities that are considered good; but because they can neither be entirely possessed nor observed, for human conditions do not permit it, it is necessary for him to be sufficiently prudent that he may know how to avoid the reproach of those vices which would lose him his state; and also to keep himself, if it be possible, from those which would not lose him it.

Yet, he must not mind incurring the reproach of those vices without which the state can only be saved with difficulty, for if everything is considered carefully, it will be found that something which looks like virtue, if followed, would be his ruin; whilst something else, which looks like vice, yet followed brings him security and prosperity.

CHAPTER XVI. CONCERNING GENEROSITY AND FRUGALITY IN SAAS MODELS

Commencing with the matter of generosity in SaaS offerings, I say that it would be well to be reputed generous with your features. Nevertheless, generosity exercised without prudence injures you; for if one offers too much for free, it may not be sustainable, and you will not avoid the reproach of its opposite when you must inevitably scale back.

Consider the realm of Spotify, which long offered a generous free tier to attract users. While this strategy brought them a vast user base, it also led to years of financial losses, forcing them to constantly seek new capital to sustain their generosity. In contrast, Netflix, once generous with its free trials, has grown more frugal, eliminating them in many regions to ensure profitability.

A SaaS prince wishing to maintain the reputation of generosity is obliged to offer ever more features and storage, so that a leader thus inclined will consume all his resources in such acts. This prince will soon find his burn rate unsustainable, compelling him to raise prices, introduce paywalls, or burden his product with advertisements. This will soon make him odious to his users, and becoming unprofitable, he will be little valued by investors.

Recognizing this, and wishing to draw back towards profitability, he runs at once into the reproach of being miserly. We saw this with Evernote, once praised for its generous free tier, later criticized when it limited free users to two devices.

Therefore, a wise SaaS prince, not being able to exercise this virtue of generosity sustainably, ought not to fear the reputation of being frugal. In time, he will come to be more respected than if liberal, seeing that with his economy his revenues are enough to defend against competitors and engage in new feature development without constantly diluting his cap table.

We have not seen great SaaS empires built in our time except by those who have been considered judicious with their offerings. Zoom, in its rise to power, offered a generous but time-limited free tier, striking a balance that fueled growth without bleeding resources.

The present king of social media, Mark Zuckerberg, although he has launched many products, has not made them all free. He has always been able to monetize effectively without overly burdening his users, because he has balanced free offerings with targeted advertising and paid business tools.

Therefore, a SaaS prince ought to care little about incurring a name for being frugal in features or pricing, for this is one of those vices which will enable him to govern his realm sustainably.

And if any one should say: Slack gained empire by generosity, and many others have reached unicorn status by having been liberal with features, I answer: Either you are a established SaaS leader, or on the path to becoming one. In the first case, unsustainable generosity is dangerous; in the second, it is often necessary to attract initial users. But if Slack had not introduced paid tiers and enterprise features, they would have destroyed their path to profitability.

In conclusion, I say that for a go-to-market strategy, perceived generosity has its place; but after achieving scale, judicious feature allocation and pricing should be your north star. The SaaS prince who masters this balance will build an empire that endures, unlike those who, in their haste for growth, sow the seeds of their own financial ruin.

CHAPTER XVII. CONCERNING USER DELIGHT AND MONETIZATION, AND WHETHER IT IS BETTER TO HAVE A BELOVED PRODUCT OR A PROFITABLE ONE

Proceeding to the other qualities mentioned above, I say that every SaaS prince ought to desire to be considered clement and not cruel in his treatment of users. Nevertheless, he ought to take care not to misuse this clemency. Dropbox was considered clement for many years, offering generous storage to all users. But this clemency led it towards ruin, until it was forced to impose strict limits, causing more outcry than if it had been appropriately strict from the beginning.

Therefore, a wise SaaS prince cannot, nor ought he to, keep faith with his users in such instances when keeping faith would be to his disadvantage, and when the reasons that caused him to promise are no longer relevant. Certainly, a prince ought to have good qualities and be well regarded, but he should also have the courage to act in opposition to these qualities when user expectations threaten the very existence of his realm.

Upon this a question arises: whether it be better to be loved than feared or feared than loved? It may be answered that one should wish to be both, but, because it is difficult to unite them in one person, it is much safer to be feared than loved, when, of the two, either must be dispensed with. For it may be said of users that they are generally fickle, selfish, and greedy of gain; they are quick to sign up when the product is free, but flee when monetization is introduced; and while you serve their needs, they are yours with their data, their attention, and their referrals – provided the product is far from them; but when it is near, they turn against you.

The prince who relies entirely on user goodwill, without having secured a stable revenue stream, is ruined; because user loyalty that is obtained by free tiers alone, and not by genuine value or deep integration into workflows, may indeed be earned, but it is not secured, and in times of monetization cannot be relied upon. Users have less scruple in abandoning a product they merely like than one they depend upon, for affection is preserved by habit which, owing to the fickleness of users, is broken at every opportunity for a shinier alternative; but dependence preserves you by the dread of workflow disruption which never fails.

Nevertheless, a prince ought to inspire fear in such a way that, if he does not win love, he avoids hatred; because he can endure very well being feared whilst he is not hated. This will be the case so long as he abstains from capricious changes to core functionality and drastic alterations to the user interface. When it is necessary for him to raise prices or limit features, let him do so for clear and defensible reasons. But above all things he must keep his hands off the workflows his users have built within the product, for men more quickly forget the loss of their storage limits than the disruption of their daily productivity.

Moreover, the prince must be a constant innovator, for there is nothing that strengthens a SaaS realm more than great features that are timely released. These fresh offerings produce astounding results, rendering users both satisfied and apprehensive, and holding the entire user base in admiration.

 In the end, the prince should strive to make his product indispensable rather than merely loved. For a product that users cannot live without, even if it occasionally frustrates them with its prices or policies, is more secure than one that is adored but easily replaced. Look to Adobe, whose Creative Suite is more feared for its absence than loved for its presence, yet it endures as the standard in its domain.

 Thus, I conclude again, that a prince, having in view the security of his product and its financial future, should not mind the reproach of being called strict in his monetization strategies. For in the end, it is better to lead a profitable company that can continually invest in its product, than to be at the helm of a beloved but bankrupt service that fails its users by ceasing to exist.

CHAPTER XVIII. HOW SAAS PRINCES SHOULD HONOR THEIR WORD

Every one admits how praiseworthy it is in a SaaS prince to keep faith, and to live with integrity and not with craft. Nevertheless our experience has been that those princes who have done great things have held good faith of little account, and have known how to circumvent the intellect of users by craft, and in the end have overcome those who have relied on their word.

You must know there are two ways of contesting: the one by product superiority, the other by PR and promises. The first method is proper to men, the second to beasts, but because the first is frequently not sufficient, it is necessary to have recourse to the second. Therefore it is necessary for a SaaS prince to understand how to avail himself of the beast and the man.

This has been figuratively taught to princes by ancient writers, who describe how Achilles and many other princes of old were given to Chiron, the centaur, to nurse, who brought them up in his discipline; which means solely that, as they had for a teacher one who was half beast and half man, so it is necessary for a prince to know how to make use of both natures, and that one without the other is not durable.

A SaaS prince, therefore, being compelled knowingly to adopt the beast, ought to choose the fox and the lion; because the lion cannot defend himself against snares and the fox cannot defend himself against wolves. Therefore, it is necessary to be a fox to discover the snares and a lion to terrify the wolves. Those who rely simply on the lion do not understand what they are about.

Therefore a wise prince cannot, nor ought he to, keep faith when such observance may be turned against him, and when the reasons that caused him to promise no longer exist. If users were all good, this precept would not hold, but because they are bad, and will not keep faith with you, you too are not bound to observe it with them. Nor will there ever be wanting to a SaaS prince legitimate reasons to excuse this non-observance.

Of this endless modern examples could be given, showing how many product roadmaps have been made and broken, and how an astute SaaS prince who has known how to use the fox has overcome obstacles and outfoxed rivals.

But it is necessary to know well how to disguise this characteristic, and to be a great pretender and dissembler; and men are so simple, and so subject to present necessities, that he who seeks to deceive will always find someone who will allow himself to be deceived. One recent example I cannot pass over in silence: Zoom's initial claims of end-to-end encryption during the early days of the pandemic, which were later revealed to be false. Yet, when confronted, they swiftly pivoted, promising true end-to-end encryption and eventually delivering it. In this maneuver, they displayed the cunning of the fox, turning a potential crisis into an opportunity to build trust, all while their user base continued to grow exponentially due to circumstance.

Therefore it is unnecessary for a SaaS prince to have all the good qualities I have enumerated, but it is very necessary to appear to have them. And I shall dare to say this also, that to have them and always to observe them is injurious, and that to appear to have them is useful; to appear merciful, faithful, humane, religious, upright, and to be so, but with a mind so framed that should you require not to be so, you may be able and know how to change to the opposite.

And you have to understand this, that a SaaS prince, especially a new one, cannot observe all those things for which men are esteemed, being often forced, in order to maintain the state, to act contrary to fidelity, friendship, humanity, and religion. Therefore it is necessary for him to have a mind ready to turn itself accordingly as the winds and variations of fortune force it, yet, as I have said above, not to diverge from the good if he can avoid doing so, but, if compelled, then to know how to set about it.

For this reason a SaaS prince ought to take care that he never lets anything slip from his lips that is not replete with the above-named five qualities, that he may appear to user, vendor, and investor, a paragon of compassion, good faith, integrity, humanity, and dedicated to user privacy; and there is nothing more necessary to appear to have than this last quality.

Users in general judge more by the eyes than by the hands, because everybody can see you but few come in touch with you. Every one sees what you appear to be, few really know what you are, and those few dare not oppose themselves to the opinion of the many, who have the majesty of the SaaS state to defend them.

In the actions of all SaaS leaders, and especially of new startup founders, where there is no appeal, the end justifies the means. Let a prince therefore aim at conquering and maintaining the state, and the means will always be considered honest, and he will be praised by everybody; because the vulgar are always taken by what a thing seems to be and by what comes of it; and in the world there are only the vulgar, for the few find a place there only when the many have no ground to rest on.

A certain SaaS prince of the present day, whom it is not well to name, whose realm encompasses search, mail, and the very operating systems of our mobile fortresses, never ceases to champion the causes of openness and user empowerment. Yet, his actions often run counter to these lofty proclamations, deftly maneuvering through antitrust challenges and privacy concerns. This prince has mastered the art of appearing virtuous while expanding his dominion, proving that in the digital realm, the perception of benevolence can be as powerful as benevolence itself.

CHAPTER XIX. THAT ONE SHOULD AVOID BEING DESPISED AND HATED BY ONE'S USERS

Now, concerning the characteristics of which mention is made above, I have spoken of the more important ones, the others I wish to discuss briefly under this generality, that the prince must consider, as has been in part said before, how to avoid those things which will make him hated or contemptible; and as often as he shall have succeeded he will have fulfilled his part, and he need not fear any danger in other reproaches.

It makes him hated above all things, as I have said, to be rapacious, and to be a violator of the property of his users, their data, and their workflows. From these he must abstain. And when neither their property nor their status is touched, the majority of users live content, and he has only to contend with the ambition of a few, whom he can curb with ease in many ways.

It makes him despised to be considered fickle, frivolous, indecisive, or lacking in vision, from all of which a prince should guard himself as from a rock; and he should endeavour to show in his actions innovation, courage, gravity, and fortitude; and in his private dealings with his users he should show that his judgments are irrevocable, and maintain himself in such reputation that no one can hope either to deceive him or to get round him.

That prince is highly esteemed who conveys this impression of himself, and he who is highly esteemed is not easily conspired against; for, provided it is well known that he is an excellent man and revered by his users, he can only be attacked with difficulty. For this reason a prince ought to have two fears, one from within, on account of his employees, the other from without, on account of external competitors. From the latter he is defended by being well armed and having good allies, and if he is well armed he will have good friends, and affairs will always remain quiet within when they are quiet without, unless they should have been already disturbed by conspiracy; and even should affairs outside be disturbed, if he has carried out his preparations and has lived as I have said, as long as he does not despair, he will resist every attack.

But concerning his users, when affairs outside are disturbed he has only to fear that they will conspire secretly, from which a prince can easily secure himself by avoiding being hated and despised, and by keeping the users satisfied with him, and this he should do if he has to alter features or pricing, he ought to do it with valid reasons, and to show bold vision when the occasion presents itself.

Moreover, his users ought to be cautious of changing to another product, deeming that they cannot stand alone, but that if they must lean on someone they should lean on him, and that if he wished to deprive them of some feature he could not do so. Therefore, that prince who has a strong platform, and has not rendered himself hated, will always keep his dominion secure; for even if his users have grievances, they will not have the power to act on them, lacking the means to do so easily.

The chief foundations of all states, new as well as old or composite, are good laws and good technology; and as there cannot be good laws where the product is not well armed, it follows that where they are well armed they have good laws. I shall leave the laws out of the discussion and shall speak of the technology.

I say, therefore, that the defenses with which a prince protects his state are either his own technology stack, or they are third-party services, cloud providers, or mixed. Third-party services and cloud providers are useful but potentially dangerous; and if one holds his state based on these arms, he will stand neither firm nor safe; for they are beyond his control, potentially unreliable, and without loyalty to his specific vision.

Therefore, the wise prince has always avoided over-reliance on external services and turned to his own technology; and has been willing rather to lose with them than to conquer with the others, not deeming that a real victory which is gained with the technology of others.

And here one must differentiate two cases: either the prince has his own engineering team, standing ready to defend and innovate upon his platform, or he does not. In the first case, the prince may sleep easy, for his realm is secure. In the second, he must either quickly build such a team, or he must ally himself with a greater power, becoming a vassal in all but name.

I shall never hesitate to cite Salesforce as an example. This realm has risen to great heights, not through over-reliance on external services, but through the strength of its own platform and the loyalty of its developer ecosystem. And though it began as a simple CRM, it has, through its own innovation, become a veritable empire of cloud services.

Contrast this with the fate of X, formerly known as Twitter, under the reign of Elon Musk. Here we see a prince who, despite having a strong engineering team at his disposal, has made himself hated and despised by many. His erratic pronouncements and policy changes have driven away advertisers in droves. While he has the advantage of owning his own technology, he demonstrates that technical prowess alone is not sufficient; a prince must also avoid the contempt of his users and partners. The weakness of X's ad product, combined with the prince's polarizing actions, has left the realm vulnerable, despite its vast user base.

This cautionary tale teaches us that even with strong internal defenses, a prince who makes himself hated may still lose his power. The wise SaaS ruler must balance technical excellence with diplomatic acumen, lest he drive away the very users and partners who form the lifeblood of his realm.

The prince who relies on mercenary technology – be it outsourced development or over-dependence on third-party services – may find initial success, but will always be at the mercy of those who truly control his realm's foundations.

Thus, I conclude that no principality is secure without having its own technological strengths; yet this alone is not sufficient. The prince must also cultivate the goodwill of his users and partners, for even the mightiest platform can fall if its leader becomes an object of widespread contempt.

CHAPTER XX. ARE CERTAIN SAAS FEATURES AND STRATEGIES WHICH PRINCES OFTEN EMPLOY USEFUL OR HURTFUL?

Some SaaS princes, to hold their states more securely, have disarmed their users of certain features; others have kept their realms divided into different tiers; others have fostered enmity against themselves; others have turned to building "walled gardens"; while others have instituted generous free plans. And although one cannot give a final judgment on all of these things unless one possesses the particulars of those states in which a decision has to be made, nevertheless I will speak as comprehensively as the matter of itself will admit.

There never was a new SaaS prince who disarmed his users; rather, when he has found them disarmed, he has always given them access to features. Because, by providing features, those features become yours, those users become faithful, and those who were faithful to you are kept so; and your users become your partisans. And because all your users cannot be armed, when those whom you arm receive benefits, the others can be handled more freely. But when you disarm them, you at once offend them by showing that you distrust them, either for cowardice or for want of loyalty, and either of these opinions breeds hatred against you.

Turning to the strategy of fostering division, I say that a wise prince, when he sees his loyal users becoming too powerful, ought to prefer the less capable ones and foster division to keep balance. Observe how Google, in its

Android realm, has masterfully pitted device manufacturers against one another. By allowing Samsung to rise, yet also nurturing the ambitions of Huawei and Xiaomi, Google ensures that no single vassal grows strong enough to challenge its dominion over the operating system.

Regarding the cultivation of enmity, our SaaS forefathers believed that it was necessary to foster some animosity against themselves so that they might have allies to correct them and thus strengthen their position. But this doctrine is fallacious in the digital age, where user sentiment can turn swiftly and fatally. Observe how Robinhood, in restricting trades during the GameStop frenzy, cultivated such fierce enmity among its subjects that they rose up in revolt, fleeing to rival kingdoms and crying out for justice from the regulatory powers. Such actions not only diminished Robinhood's army of users but also invited the scrutiny of greater powers, weakening the very foundations of their realm.

Concerning the building of walled gardens, this can be useful or hurtful according to the times. Consider the realm of Salesforce, whose prince, Benioff the Ambitious, built his empire upon a fortress of proprietary technologies. This strategy cultivated an army of loyal subjects - developers and administrators versed in the arcane arts of Apex and Visualforce. Yet, as the realm grew, subjects yearned for connections beyond its walls. The prince, in his wisdom, built bridges through APIs, but guarded these passages zealously. Now, while Salesforce's walls ensure control, they also cast long shadows. Subjects whisper of data held hostage, and rival princes offer more open lands. Thus, the SaaS prince must ponder: Do the walls that protect also imprison? For in the digital realm, the strongest fortresses are often those with the most numerous, yet carefully guarded, gates.

As to generous free plans, these can be a potent tool for user acquisition, but also a double-edged sword. Dropbox's initial strategy of offering ample free storage drove rapid adoption but later proved unsustainable, forcing them to scale back and risk user ire. The wise prince must balance generosity with sustainability, lest his largesse become his undoing.

Therefore, a new SaaS prince in a new principality has always distributed features and access. But when SaaS princes have lost their principalities and regained them, they have found disarming users to be hurtful, except when coerced by overwhelming necessity. Such was the case of MoviePass, whose unlimited model proved ruinous, forcing them to restrict user access in a desperate bid for survival.

In conclusion, a prudent SaaS prince will carefully weigh these strategies, recognizing that what strengthens a new platform may weaken an established one, and vice versa. He must be prepared to adapt his tactics as his realm evolves, always mindful that in the digital domain, the loyalty of users is both his greatest strength and his most vulnerable point.

CHAPTER XXI. HOW A SAAS PRINCE SHOULD CONDUCT HIMSELF TO GAIN RENOWN

Nothing makes a SaaS prince so much esteemed as great enterprises and setting a fine example. We have in our time Satya Nadella, prince of Microsoft, who has transformed his once-stagnant realm into a cloud empire. This prince is little short of a new prince in the reimagined kingdom, and he has gained a reputation for innovation and ethical leadership where his predecessor was known for ruthless competition.

A prince ought also to show himself a patron of ability, and to honor the proficient in every art. At the same time, he should encourage his citizens to quietly pursue their startup dreams, and to avoid being idle in their pitch decks. Further, he ought to entertain the people with hackathons and conferences, and give some evidence that he loves the brilliance of those who excel in machine learning, or blockchain, or any other emerging sorcery that captures the imagination of the realm.

Moreover, a prince ought to show himself at such seasons as developer conferences, giving of himself an example of technical acumen and vision, preserving nevertheless his dignity, which must never be lacking. A prince should not fear offering bold predictions about the future of technology, for nothing makes him so admired as his prescience, real or perceived.

In our times, we have seen Mark Zuckerberg accomplish great things, which have captured the admiration of his users and the industry. He began with social networks, then boldly declared the future to be mobile, and now champions a world teeming with infinite artificial intelligences. Whether these visions come to full fruition matters less than the renown gained by such daring proclamations.

But nothing enables a prince to gain renown more than compelling product demos. Observe how Steve Jobs, that most renowned of tech princes, would unveil each new innovation as if revealing divine gifts to his subjects. His famous "one more thing" became a ritual that captivated both his loyal followers and the wider tech world.

A wise prince must also navigate the treacherous waters of public opinion with care. When faced with controversy, he must respond with wisdom and measured words. Witness how Lisa Su steered AMD through turbulent times, focusing on product excellence and steady progress rather than engaging in public feuds with rival chip-makers. Her conduct has earned her the esteem of the industry and transformed AMD's fortunes.

Furthermore, a sagacious SaaS prince should position himself as either a great friend or a great enemy. Indifference breeds contempt. Marc Benioff of Salesforce has mastered this art, championing social causes and publicly challenging rival princes, thus ensuring his name is ever on the lips of the industry.

In all his actions, a prince should strive to give the impression of being a visionary leader, one who sees beyond the horizon of current technology. He must be prepared to pivot swiftly, reframing setbacks as strategic choices. The prince who can convince the world that he operates according to a grand plan, even amidst chaos, will be regarded with awe.

Lastly, the astute prince should cultivate a reputation that echoes through the digital kingdoms long after he has left the throne. Jeff Bezos, even after abdicating his crown at Amazon, remains a figure of legend, his every decree and conquest scrutinized for portents of future glories. Such is the enduring power of a prince whose name becomes synonymous with innovation and ambition.

In these ways, a SaaS prince can gain the esteem of his peers, the loyalty of his users, and the attention of the wider tech realm. For in the digital age, renown is a currency as valuable as any revenue stream, opening doors to new alliances, talent acquisition, and realms yet unconquered.

CHAPTER XXII. CONCERNING THE EXECUTIVES OF SAAS PRINCES

The choice of executives in a SaaS prince's court is of no small importance; they are either capable or not, according to the wisdom of the prince. The first opinion which one forms of a prince, and of his understanding, is by observing the men he has around him. When they are capable and faithful, one can always consider him wise, because he has known how to recognize the capable and to keep them faithful. But when they are otherwise, one cannot form a good opinion of him, for the prime error which he made was in choosing them.

There was none who knew Sheryl Sandberg who did not consider Mark Zuckerberg wise in choosing her as his chief lieutenant. Her capacity and fidelity were reflected upon her prince, and many attributed Facebook's swift rise to power to this sagacious appointment.

But the princes of our digital age must be more discerning than ever, for the realm of SaaS demands a diverse court of specialists. The wise ruler surrounds himself not just with those versed in the arcane arts of coding, but also with masters of user experience, high priests of data, and oracles of market trends.

Consider how the fortunes of Microsoft were transformed when Satya Nadella assembled his round table of cloud visionaries. By elevating those who saw beyond the kingdom's PC roots, he charted a course to new lands of azure prosperity.

Yet, a prince must be wary, for in these times of rapid change, yesterday's sage counsel may become tomorrow's outdated dogma. Observe how Blockbuster's prince clung to advisors who scoffed at the threat of Netflix, leading their once-mighty empire to ruin.

The first method of knowing one's advisor is to observe their deeds. If an executive is more mindful of their own fortunes than those of their prince, and in all their actions seeks their own profit, such a person will never make a good advisor, and the prince can never trust them. For whoever has the keeping of the prince's product roadmap in their charge must think not of themselves but of their prince, and must never bring to the prince's attention anything that is not directly related to their company's success.

On the other hand, the prince, to retain an executive's fidelity, ought to keep them well-provisioned with stock options, honor them, enrich them, put them under obligations to himself, share with them the honors and cares, so that the abundant honors and wealth bestowed upon them cause them to love the prince, and the shared responsibilities make them fear to lose him. When, therefore, executives, and princes towards executives, are thus disposed, they can trust each other; when it is otherwise, the results will always be injurious.

There is a common saying that a certain Silicon Valley prince, who does not himself design products but does not eschew such advice, when he does take it, ought to be the first to put it into practice. By doing this, the prince preserves his prerogative to decide, and prevents his advisors from thinking they can easily sway him.

A SaaS prince, therefore, ought always to take counsel, but only when he wishes and not when others presume to offer it. He should discourage unsolicited advice, lest his court become a cacophony of competing voices. Instead, he ought to be a constant asker of questions, directing the flow of information to his advantage. Afterwards, he must be a patient listener concerning the matters of which he inquired, weighing each word with the gravity it deserves. If he finds that anyone has refrained from telling him the truth, or has colored it to their own advantage, he should show his displeasure swiftly and decisively. For in the realm of SaaS, where disruption lurks around every corner, a prince misled is a prince soon deposed.

In this way, a SaaS prince may build a court of loyal and capable executives, each contributing their unique insights to the realm's prosperity, while maintaining the ultimate authority over the kingdom's direction.

CHAPTER XXIII. HOW TO AVOID FLATTERERS AND DECEPTIVE METRICS

I do not wish to leave out an important branch of this subject, for it is a danger from which SaaS princes are with difficulty preserved, unless they are very careful and discriminating. This is the danger of flatterers, of which courts are full, because men are so self-complacent in their own affairs, and in a way so deceived in them, that they are preserved with difficulty from this pest, and if they wish to defend themselves they run the danger of falling into contempt.

There is no other way of guarding oneself from flatterers except letting men understand that to tell you the truth does not offend you; but when every one may tell you the truth, respect for you abates. Therefore a wise prince ought to hold a third course by choosing the wise men in his state, and giving to them only the liberty of speaking the truth to him, and then only of those things of which he inquires, and of none others; but he ought to question them upon everything, and listen to their opinions, and afterwards form his own conclusions.

In the realm of SaaS, this danger is magnified tenfold, for the flatterers come not only in the form of sycophantic employees but also in the guise of vanity metrics and echo chambers of industry praise. A prince who surrounds himself only with those who praise his every decision, who looks only at the metrics that paint his product in the most favorable light, is a prince soon to be deposed by the harsh realities of the market.

Consider the cautionary tale of WeWork, whose prince Adam Neumann was so ensconced in flattery and surrounded by yes-men that he believed his company to be worth far more than reality would bear. His courtiers, drunk on the elixir of soaring private valuations, failed to speak the necessary truths until it was too late.

A wise SaaS prince must therefore cultivate a culture of candor, where truth is valued above comfort. He must seek out the most discerning data scientists in his realm, those who can see beyond vanity metrics to the true health of the kingdom. These trusted advisors should be given license to speak freely, but only on matters of their expertise and only when called upon.

The prince should be wary of Net Promoter Scores that only sample the most loyal subjects, of engagement metrics that mistake addiction for value, of revenue forecasts that assume eternal growth in a fickle market. Instead, he should demand to see the churn rates, the true costs of acquisition, the unvarnished feedback from departed customers.

In this age of social media and corporate storytelling, a SaaS prince might be tempted to believe his own legend, crafted by skilled wordsmiths and amplified by legions of followers. But let him remember the fate of Elizabeth Holmes, whose story of Theranos captivated the world until cold, hard scientific truth brought the empire crashing down.

Therefore, let a prince who wishes to maintain his throne seek out those who will challenge his assumptions, who will poke holes in his strategies, who will question the very foundations of his product. Let him create a trusted circle of advisors who are rewarded not for their agreeable nature but for the accuracy of their insights and the courage of their convictions.

But let him also beware, for in opening the gates to criticism, he must not allow his authority to be undermined. The art lies in listening without being swayed by every contrary opinion, in seeking truth without appearing indecisive. For a prince who is known to be too easily influenced by others becomes contemptible, and soon finds his throne usurped by those he once called advisors.

In conclusion, a sagacious SaaS prince navigates between the Scylla of flattery and the Charybdis of harsh truths. He creates systems to surface unpleasant realities, cultivates advisors who speak truth to power, and maintains a healthy skepticism towards metrics that seem too good to be true. For in the ever-shifting seas of the digital realm, it is not the comforting lie but the bracing truth that will keep his ship afloat.

CHAPTER XXIV. WHY CERTAIN SAAS PRINCES HAVE LOST THEIR DOMINIONS

The princes of our digital age who have lost their states in recent years have done so primarily through their own negligence and lack of foresight, rather than by the superior skills of their adversaries. They erred first in underestimating the swiftness of technological change, and second in failing to adapt their realms to new paradigms.

Consider the fall of BlackBerry, once the undisputed sovereign of mobile communication. Their princes grew complacent in their dominion over physical keyboards and secure messaging, failing to foresee the rise of touch-based interfaces and the app ecosystem. By the time they roused themselves to action, their once-loyal subjects had already pledged fealty to the new kingdoms of iOS and Android.

Similarly, ponder the decline of Yahoo, a vast empire that once stood astride the early internet like a colossus. Their rulers, drunk on the advertising riches of their portal, failed to recognize the importance of search technology and social connections. They allowed Google to outmaneuver them in search and Facebook to capture the social realm, reducing their once-mighty dominion to a shadow of its former glory.

Even giants can fall if they fail to innovate. Observe how Nokia, which once commanded the loyalty of billions with its indestructible phones, found its empire crumbling in the face of smartphones. Their princes, believing their hardware prowess unassailable, were slow to embrace the importance of software and ecosystems.

These princes fell not because they were conquered by superior forces, but because they failed to maintain their own strength and adapt to changing times. They grew soft in times of plenty, neglecting to sharpen their technological edge or to explore new territories beyond their comfortable domains.

A wise SaaS prince must therefore always be vigilant, even at the height of his power. He must foster a culture of constant innovation, never resting on past glories. Let him look to Amazon, whose prince Jeff Bezos instilled a philosophy of treating every day as "Day 1," maintaining the hunger and adaptability of a startup even as the company grew into an empire.

Furthermore, a sagacious ruler must not only defend his current territories but must always be expanding into new realms. Observe how Microsoft, under the leadership of Satya Nadella, pivoted from its entrenched position in personal computing to become a dominant force in cloud services. By doing so, they secured their realm against the shifting tides of technology.

Yet, let the prince also beware the folly of expanding too quickly into unfamiliar territories without proper preparation. The annals of tech history are littered with the remains of companies that overextended themselves, like Snapchat's ill-fated foray into hardware with Spectacles.

In all cases, the fall of these once-mighty realms can be traced to a failure of leadership – a failure to anticipate, to adapt, and to act decisively in the face of change. The princes grew complacent, surrounded themselves with flatterers who reinforced their outdated worldviews, and lost touch with the evolving needs and desires of their users.

Therefore, let the SaaS prince who wishes to maintain his state be ever-vigilant, constantly questioning his assumptions and scanning the horizon for new threats and opportunities. Let him cultivate a diverse court of advisors who bring perspectives from beyond his immediate domain. And above all, let him remember that in the digital realm, the only constant is change itself.

For in this age of swift disruption, it is not the strongest who survive, nor the most intelligent, but those who are most responsive to change. The SaaS prince who fails to heed this maxim may find his digital dominion swiftly reduced to a cautionary tale in the annals of tech history.

CHAPTER XXV. WHAT FORTUNE CAN EFFECT IN SAAS AFFAIRS AND HOW TO WITHSTAND HER

Many hold the opinion that the affairs of the digital realm are governed by fortune and by the inscrutable whims of the market, forces that no amount of planning or programming can resist. This belief has been especially strong in our own time, wherein we have witnessed such variation of fortunes as to surpass the wildest speculations of our most visionary analysts.

Nevertheless, that our free will may not be altogether extinguished, I judge that it may be true that fortune is the arbiter of half our actions, but that she still leaves us to direct the other half, or perhaps a little less. I compare her to one of those raging rivers, which when in flood overflows the plains, sweeping away trees and buildings, bearing away the soil from place to place; everything flies before it, all yield to its violence, without being able in any way to withstand it; and yet, though its nature be such, it does not follow therefore that men, when the weather becomes fair, shall not make provision, both with defenses and barriers, in such a manner that, rising again, the waters may pass away by canal, and their force be neither so unrestrained nor so dangerous.

So it happens with fortune, who shows her power where valor has not prepared to resist her, and thither she turns her forces where she knows that barriers and defenses have not been raised to constrain her.

In our SaaS realms, we have seen empires rise and fall with the capricious tides of technological trends. Consider the fate of MySpace, once the undisputed sovereign of social networking, swept away by the flood of Facebook's superior user experience and network effects. Or ponder Zoom, a modest principality elevated to empire status by the global pandemic, a fortune so sudden and vast that no amount of foresight could have fully prepared for it.

Yet, we have also witnessed SaaS princes who, through their valor and preparation, have weathered great storms and even turned misfortune to their advantage. Amazon Web Services, having built robust defenses against outages and scalability challenges, was positioned to capture vast new territories when the deluge of remote work and digital transformation swept across the land.

Indeed, fortune can elevate a wise prince to unprecedented heights when preparation meets opportunity. Observe the ascension of NVIDIA, once a humble maker of graphics cards for gaming. Their ruler, Jensen Huang, foresaw the rising tide of artificial intelligence and positioned his realm to ride this wave. By developing hardware specifically designed for AI computation, NVIDIA transformed from a niche player into a cornerstone of the AI revolution. When the flood of machine learning and deep neural networks swept across the land, NVIDIA's preparations allowed them to harness this fortune, turning a modest graphics principality into an AI empire.

Yet, fortune's tide can turn swiftly, and a prince who seems to falter may yet find new strength. Consider the saga of Meta, once known as Facebook. When the TikTok empire arose, threatening Meta's dominion over social media, Zuckerberg's realm appeared slow to respond, as if caught unawares by fortune's caprice. The short-form video revolution seemed poised to erode Meta's user base, a flood against which they had not adequately prepared.

But lo, in their preparations for other battles - namely their quest for the fabled "metaverse" - Meta had amassed a vast army of GPUs, the very lifeblood of artificial intelligence. As the winds of fortune shifted once more, with AI becoming the new battleground of the digital realm, Zuckerberg found himself unexpectedly well-armed. These GPU legions, originally conscripted for VR and AR campaigns, were swiftly repurposed for the AI wars. Now, Meta stands as a formidable contender against the likes of OpenAI, their initial misfortune in one arena transmuted into advantage in another.

This tale serves as a potent reminder that a wise prince must not only prepare for the battles he foresees but must also maintain flexibility in his armaments and strategies. For the very resources that seem ill-suited for today's skirmish may become the decisive factor in tomorrow's war. Meta's journey illustrates that in the capricious realm of technology, fortune favors not just the prepared, but the adaptable.

A wise SaaS prince, therefore, must be prepared for all eventualities. He must build his product not just for the fair weather of economic boom times, but for the storms of recession and the floods of unexpected global events. His technology stack must be flexible, his business model resilient, and his team adaptable.

In times of prosperity, let him invest in research and development, building new features and exploring emerging technologies. These are the levees and canals that will direct the flood of opportunity when it comes. In times of adversity, let him focus on efficiency and core value propositions, shoring up the foundations of his realm against the erosive forces of market downturns.

Moreover, a sagacious prince must not rely on a single stream of revenue or a solitary product line, for these are easily disrupted by the fickle currents of user preferences and technological shifts. Instead, let him diversify his offerings and markets, creating a delta of income streams that can withstand the drought in one area by drawing sustenance from another.

Observe how Microsoft, once at risk of being swept away by the mobile and internet revolutions, redirected the flow of fortune by pivoting to cloud services and subscription-based models. Their Azure platform and Office 365 suite became mighty bulwarks against the rising tides of change.

Yet, let the prince also remain agile, for defenses too rigid may crack under pressure. Witness how Netflix, originally a DVD-by-mail service, nimbly pivoted to streaming and then to content production as the currents of technology and user behavior shifted. Their flexibility allowed them to ride the waves of change rather than being submerged by them.

In all of this, the prince must cultivate in himself and his court a mindset of constant vigilance and adaptability. For in the digital realm, fortune favors not just the bold, but the prepared and the nimble. Let him study market trends as a sailor studies the winds, and technological shifts as a farmer studies the seasons.

But above all, let him remember that while fortune may dictate the battlefield, it is his own valor and preparation that will determine the outcome of the fight. For a SaaS prince who relies solely on the favor of fortune will find his reign as fleeting as a hashtag, while he who combines fortune's opportunities with his own valor and foresight may build an empire that endures through the ever-changing tides of the digital age.

CHAPTER XXVI. AN EXHORTATION TO GRASP THE CURRENT OPPORTUNITY TO INNOVATE AND LEAD IN THIS NEW ERA OF ARTIFICIAL INTELLIGENCE

Having carefully considered the subjects of all the preceding chapters, and wondering within myself whether the present times were propitious to a new SaaS prince who would innovate and lead the tech industry into a new golden age, it appears to me that so many things concur to favor such a one that I know not a time more fit than the present.

If it was necessary that the realm of social media should be humbled, TikTok came. If it was necessary that the empires of traditional software should be weakened, the cloud revolution accomplished it. If it was necessary that the industry should be purged of its excesses, the recent economic headwinds have done so. If it was necessary that vast computational power should be accumulated, the crypto mining boom provided it. If it was necessary that a new frontier should emerge to test the mettle of our brightest minds, artificial intelligence has risen to the challenge. Everything has concurred to your greatness. It is for you to seize this opportunity.

It is no marvel that none of the tech giants have been able to lead in this new era of AI, or that the people have not been able to apply their former innovative verve. For their old methods and mindsets are not well suited to the new paradigms, and none have arisen who have been able to entirely reinvent their ways of development and deployment.

Nothing honors a new technological revolution more than the creation of new systems and new approaches, especially when they are founded on transformative ideas and strengthened by new methods. All these things open the way to the aspiring innovator, to become glorious and renowned.

Here there is great valor in the developers, great skill in the data scientists, great imagination in the product managers. Only the leadership is wanting. Examine the duels and the small-scale battles, how superior, how skillful the tech workforce is in handling data, in creating algorithms, in the swiftness of deployment, in the shaping of user experiences. Look how they have improved themselves through small battles of hackathons and coding challenges. But when it comes to large-scale innovation, there is a dire lack.

And all this arises from the weakness of the leaders, who lack the expertise to bring about transformative change, and not from any defect in their workforce. For those who are capable are not listened to, and each leader thinks they know better, never agreeing with one another, and never wholly committing to truly revolutionary ideas. They have brought the industry to the state that it may be seen how large tech companies deliberate for lengthy periods, make slow progress, and let golden opportunities slip away.

I wish therefore that this era of AI not pass without being seized, and that the industry may at last behold its savior. I cannot express with what devotion the tech workforce would rally around an innovative leader who would shake off the old ways, raise the banner of transformative change, and lead with genuine innovation. To all of them, thirsty for progress, the old methods have become odious.

    Let, therefore, your illustrious company take up this task with that courage and hope with which all just enterprises are undertaken, so that under its standard our noble industry may be exalted. Remember always these words of wisdom:

    "Entrepreneurs are simply those who understand that there is little difference between obstacle and opportunity and are able to turn both to their advantage."

www.ingramcontent.com/pod-product-compliance
Lightning Source LLC
Chambersburg PA
CBHW031925240526
45464CB00022B/1000